D1304948

CURIOUS PET PALS

MY FRIEND THE HERMIT CRAB

Joanne Randolph

WINDMILL BOOKS
New York

Published in 2011 by Windmill Books, LLC
303 Park Avenue South, Suite # 1280, New York, NY 10010-3657

First Edition

Editor: Jennifer Way
Book Design: Erica Clendening
Layout Design: Julio Gil
Photo Researcher: Ashley Burrell

Photo Credits: Cover, pp. 4, 5, 7, 13, 16, 19 Shutterstock.com; pp. 6, 14 © www.istockphoto.com/Nancy Nehring; p. 8 Georgette Douwma/Getty Images; p. 10 Reinhard Dirscherl/Visuals Unlimited, Inc./Getty Images; p. 11 © www.istockphoto.com/WinterStorm; p. 12 © www.istockphoto.com/Zando Escultura; p. 15 Joe Raedle/Getty Images; p. 17 © www.istockphoto.com/Kim Gunkel; p. 18 Wolfgang Poelzer/Peter Arnold Inc.; p. 20 © FLPA/Malcolm Schuyl/age fotostock; p. 21 William Thomas Cain/Getty Images.

Library of Congress Cataloging-in-Publication Data

Randolph, Joanne.
  My friend the hermit crab / by Joanne Randolph.
     p. cm. — (Curious pet pals)
Includes index.
ISBN 978-1-60754-978-9 (library binding) — ISBN 978-1-60754-987-1 (pbk.) — ISBN 978-1-60754-988-8 (6-pack)
1. Hermit crabs as pets—Juvenile literature. I. Title.
SF459.H47R36 2011
639'.67—dc22

                                        2010004698

Manufactured in the United States of America

For more great fiction and nonfiction, go to www.windmillbooks.com

CPSIA Compliance Information: Batch #BW2011WM: For Further Information contact Rosen Publishing, New York, New York at 1-800-237-9932

CONTENTS

MEET THE HERMIT CRAB

If you have never had a pet before, maybe you want one now. If you are thinking of getting a pet, it is important to learn about the animal you're thinking of

Hermit crabs are curious animals. This means they want to know all about their surroundings.

getting. This will help you find the right pet for you and learn how to care for it.

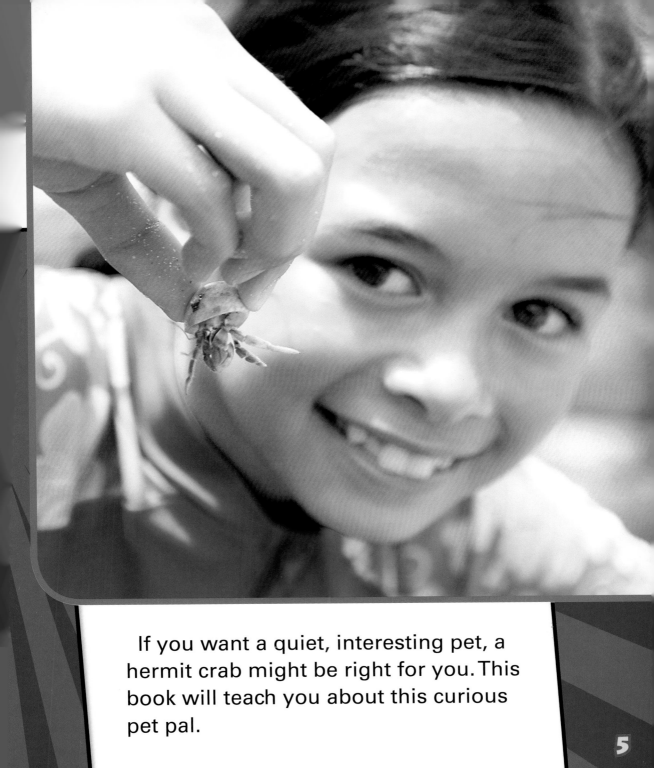

If you want a quiet, interesting pet, a hermit crab might be right for you. This book will teach you about this curious pet pal.

A hermit crab is a **crustacean**. Lobsters, shrimps, and barnacles are other crustaceans.

Here you can see the hermit crab's shell-covered legs. This shell is the exoskeleton.

Hermit crabs have ten legs. The front pair of legs are **claws**. A hermit crab has a soft belly, but the rest of its body is covered in a hard outer covering,

This is a blue crawfish. Crawfish are another kind of crustacean.

called an **exoskeleton**. This exoskeleton keeps the body safe. It also gives the body its shape. Hermit crabs don't make their shell. They find an empty shell and attach it to their body.

Most crustaceans have an exoskeleton that covers their whole body. Hermit crabs are a bit different, though. Hermit crabs have a soft **abdomen**. The abdomen is the backmost part of their body.

To keep their abdomen safe, hermit crabs borrow shells left behind by other animals. They can pull their whole body into their shell to hide from other animals!

Hermit crabs will fight other hermit crabs to take their shell. The hermit crab on the right is feeding on a dead fish.

Hermit crabs change shells as they grow. They need to find a shell to fit their larger body.

Most hermit crabs in pet stores are land hermit crabs. Caribbean hermit crabs and Ecuadorian hermit crabs are the most common land hermit crabs.

In the wild, hermit crabs may live in groups of up to 100 crabs. They walk along the beach together looking for food.

When you go to buy your hermit crabs, plan to get more than one. Hermit crabs are social. That means that they like to live in groups. If you

keep more than one pet crab, you should try to get crabs that are close in size. Bigger crabs in your tank may eat the smaller ones!

HOME FOR YOUR HERMIT CRAB

So what do you need to keep your pet hermit crab safe, healthy, and happy? A 10-gallon (40 l) glass aquarium has enough space for up to five hermit crabs to move around happily.

Your hermit crabs will like toys and places to hide in and climb on. These two hermit crabs sit on a piece of driftwood.

Hermit crabs like to burrow in the sand, so the aquarium should be filled about halfway with sand or gravel.

You need to put at least 5 inches (12 cm) of sand or gravel in the bottom of your hermit crab's aquarium.

You will need a heating pad or heat lamp for your hermit crab's home, too. The cage should be between 70 and 85° F (21–29° C).

If your hermit crab seems to be hiding, it may be **molting**. They bury themselves in the sand when they molt. They may stay buried for as long as 3 to 4 weeks!

This hermit crab has borrowed the shell of a turban snail. Hermit crab shells can be beautiful and colorful.

Hermit crabs change shells when they molt. Sometimes hermit crabs change shells even if they did not molt, so it's good to have extra shells

You can buy all kinds of painted shells for your crab. Just be sure they are not painted with anything that could hurt your crab.

in your aquarium. Don't use shells picked up from the beach. You can buy clean shells from a pet store.

CARE AND FEEDING

Hermit crabs need a **humid** home. That means they like warm and wet surroundings.

This hermit crab is resting on a beach.

Hermit crabs need freshwater for drinking. The **chemicals** in water from your sink can hurt your crab. You need to add other chemicals to tap water to make it safe for your hermit crab to

This girl is taking a close look at her hermit crab. You can use a tool, such as this magnifying glass, to check your crab for health problems, such as bugs called mites.

drink. You can buy these chemicals at the pet store. Your hermit crab also needs a saltwater pool that is big enough for it to splash around in.

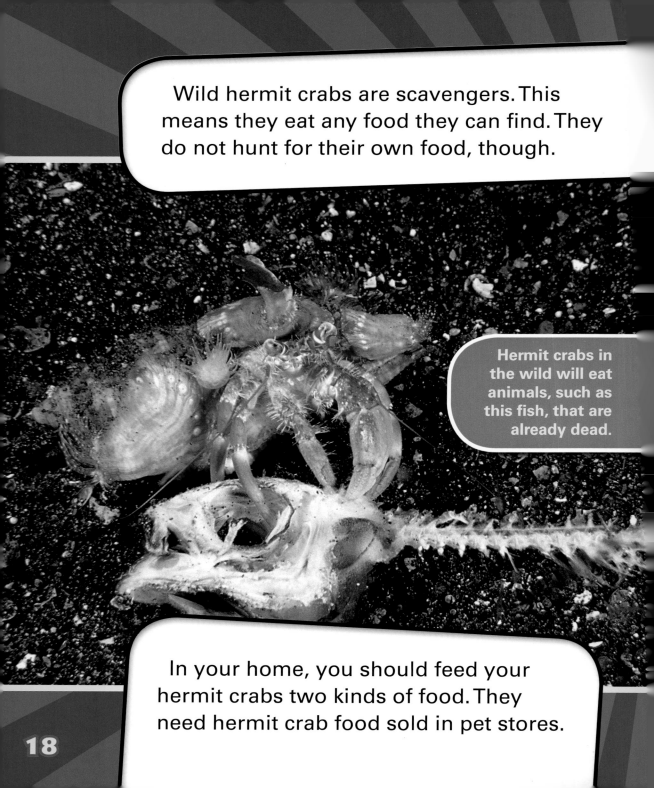

Wild hermit crabs are scavengers. This means they eat any food they can find. They do not hunt for their own food, though.

Hermit crabs in the wild will eat animals, such as this fish, that are already dead.

In your home, you should feed your hermit crabs two kinds of food. They need hermit crab food sold in pet stores.

Pet hermit crabs eat special foods that are made just for them. These are both wet and dry foods. Dry food is shown below.

They also like lots of different treats. Grapes, lettuce, plain pasta, dried shrimp, plain popcorn, and fresh fish are some good treats for a hermit crab.

Hermit crabs are not soft and cuddly pets, like cats, dogs, and hamsters are.

Don't litter at the beach. Wild hermit crabs will sometimes move into trash left behind on the beach.

Hermit crabs can be fun, though. It is interesting to watch them eat, splash, and play in their aquarium.

Owning a hermit crab is a big job. You need to give your pet what it needs to stay healthy. If you do, you can enjoy watching and learning about your new pets for a long time.

GUESS WHAT?

Hermit crabs can live anywhere from 6 to 30 years if you take good care of them.

Hermit crabs **urinate** through their antennae!

You should wash new shells and boil them in water. Then you can put them in your crab's home.

Habitat is the word for the place an animal or plant naturally lives. People who own hermit crabs call hermit crabs' cages a "crabitat."

Hermit crabs need a humid home. This means they like it to be a bit wet. If the air in their cage is too dry, the crab can die.

GLOSSARY

ABDOMEN (AB-duh-mun) The large, rear part of an insect's or arthropod's body.

CHEMICALS (KEH-mih-kulz) Matter that can be mixed with other matter to cause changes.

CRUSTACEAN (krus-TAY-shun) An animal that has no backbone, has a hard shell and other body parts, and lives mostly in water.

EXOSKELETON (ek-soh-SKEH-leh-tun) The hard covering on the outside of an animal's body that holds and guards the soft insides.

HUMID (HYOO-id) Wet and warm.

MOLTING (MOHLT-ing) Shedding hair, feathers, shell, horns, or skin.

URINATE (YER-ih-nayt) To pass liquid, or water-like, wastes from the body.

READ MORE

Fox, Sue. *Hermit Crabs: A Complete Pet Owner's Manual.* New York: Barron's Educational Series, 2000.

Pavia, Adele. *Hermit Crab: Your Happy, Healthy Pet.* New York: Howell Book House, 2006.

Richardson, Adele. *Caring for Your Hermit Crab.* Mankato, MN: Capstone Press, 2006.

INDEX

WEB SITES

For Web resources related to the subject of this book, go to: www.windmillbooks.com/weblinks and select this book's title.